GONE!
DINO EXTINCTION

Protoceratops
(pro-toe-SER-uh-tops)

3D DINOSAUR DISCOVERY™

by
Kathleen Kranking

with
Matthew T. Carrano, Ph.D.
Consultant

Scholastic Inc.

New York   Toronto   London   Auckland   Sydney
Mexico City   New Delhi   Hong Kong   Buenos Aires

ISBN 0-439-83878-9

Designer: Lee Kaplan.

Cover illustration: *T. rex, Triceratops,* and meteors © Joe Tucciarone.

Title page: *Protoceratops* © Jaime Chirinos; (desert background) © amygdala imagery/Shutterstock.com.

Back cover illustration: *Gorgosaurus* © Julius Csotonyi; (trees) © Aron Hsiao/Shutterstock.com; (road) © Joy Brown/Shutterstock.com; (people) © Alon Othnay/Shutterstock.com.

All Ty the *Tyrannosaurus rex* illustrations by Ed Shems.

All 3-D and red reveal conversions by Pinsharp 3D Graphics.

Interior Photo and Illustration Credits:
Pages 4–5: *T. rex* and supernova © Joe Tucciarone.
Pages 6–7: *Appalachiosaurus* © Todd Marshall.
Pages 8–9: *Plateosaurus* © Todd Marshall.
Pages 10–11: *Protoceratops* and skeleton illustrations © Jaime Chirinos; (desert background) © amygdala imagery/Shutterstock.com; cartoon by Ed Shems.
Pages 12–13: Spot illustrations by Robert Rath; (desert with skull) © Ximagination/Shutterstock.com.
Pages 14–15: Space rock near Earth © Joe Tucciarone; (relief image of the Yucatan peninsula) NASA-JPL.
Pages 16–17: (Erupting volcano) © Erik H. Pronske/Shutterstock.com; volcano diagram by Robert Rath.
Pages 18–19: (Supernova blast wave) NASA-HQ-GRIN; comet sailing past Earth © Joe Tucciarone.
Pages 20–23: All cartoons by Ed Shems.
Pages 24–25: Extinct animal illustrations © Stephen Missal; (Earth) R. Stockli/Robert Simmon/ NASA/GFC/MODIS; (mammal fossil) © Louie Psihoyos/Science Faction/Getty Images.
Page 26: (Chicken and *Mononykus* skeleton) © Louie Psihoyos/Science Faction/Getty Images.
Pages 27–28: *Gorgosaurus* © Julius Csotonyi; (trees) © Aron Hsiao/Shutterstock.com; (road) © Joy Brown/Shutterstock.com; (people) © Alon Othnay/Shutterstock.com.
Page 29: (Greg Wilson) © S. Anantharaman, photo courtesy of Greg Wilson; (clouds) © Gloria Ghiara/Shutterstock.com; (African scene) © Andre Klaassen/Shutterstock.com.
Pages 30–31: Illustration © Stephen Missal.
Page 32: *Maiasaura* © Todd Marshall.

12 11 10 9 8 7 6 5 4 3 2   7 8 9 10 11/0

Printed in the U.S.A.

First Scholastic printing, October 2006

TABLE OF
CONTENTS

A *T. rex* and a supernova

DINO EXTINCTION!

Hi there, it's me, Ty! Are you ready for another **3-D Dinosaur Discovery** adventure? We're going to try to solve one of the biggest mysteries of all time: what happened to the dinosaurs? We'll follow the clues scientists have found about this vanishing act and learn lots of new and exciting facts along the way! Did you know that...

Ty
Tyrannosaurus rex
(tie-RAN-oh-SOR-uhss RECKS)

◆ Some scientists think that the answer to the dinos' disappearance might come from outer space?

　　◆ There have been other big wipe-outs like the one that got the dinosaurs?

　　　　◆ Animals are disappearing every day?

And we'll try to dig up answers to questions like:

◆ What clues can scientists get about dino extinction from rocks?

　　◆ What happened to other animals when dinos disappeared?

　　◆ What would it be like if dinos lived today?

 Remember, when you see this icon, put on your **3-D glasses** to make the pictures pop!

Ready to look at the clues? Then turn the page and let's get started!

No *T. rexes?*
Too bad!

There's no question that dinosaurs are gone—you'll never see a *T. rex* stomping across your backyard!

So what happened? That's a question that has scientists scratching their heads. Scientists do know that dinos disappeared, or went **extinct** (eks-STINKT), at the end of the Cretaceous Period, 65 million years ago. But not everybody agrees on how this happened. In this book, we'll check out the clues scientists have found as they try to solve this prehistoric puzzle.

Dino Dictionary

When an animal or plant becomes *extinct*, it means no more of its kind exists anywhere in the world. It's gone forever!

First, in **The Big E**, we'll look at what extinction is and some different kinds of extinctions. Then, in **A Vanishing Act**, we'll look at the facts that scientists have found so far and investigate some of their ideas on what happened.

And in **Goofy Guesses**, we'll sneak a peek at some silly ideas that people have come up with about the dinos' disappearing act. We'll also check out the animals that survived the big wipe-out in **A Different World**. Ever wonder what life would be like if dinos were still around? We'll find out in **If Reptiles Ruled Today...**!

Appalachiosaurus
(ah-puh-LAH-cha-SOR-uhss)

We'll also learn about some of the last dinos that walked the Earth and hear what an expert has to say on dino extinction. We've got lots to cover, so let's go!

Funny Bones

Q: What comes after an extinction?

A: A Y-stinction.

Q: What comes after a Y-stinction?

A: Z-end!

THE BIG E

Did you know that there's more than one kind of extinction? It's true! Scientists group extinctions into two types: **background extinctions** and **mass extinctions**. Read on to learn more about the big E!

Fading Out

Small extinctions, where only a few **species** (SPEE-sees) die out at a time, are called *background extinctions*. In background extinction, the number of a group of plants or animals gets smaller and smaller over millions and millions of years. After a while, the whole group of animals or plants dies out and goes extinct. Believe it or not, background extinction is going on all the time—even as you're reading this book!

Life Goes On

Why do species start disappearing? Animals go extinct because they can't survive changes in their surroundings. These changes might be the weather heating up, or maybe other animals coming along and eating all the food. If animals can **adapt** (uh-DAPT) by eating something else, or being able to sweat out the warmer weather, then they live on. If they can't adapt to the changes, they slowly die out over a long period of time and go extinct.

Not a Big Bummer

Extinction might seem like a bummer, but it's a part of life. And it isn't all bad! Extinction helps make room for new plants and animals that are appearing all the time. Just think about it: if all the plants and animals that ever lived on Earth for the last 3½ billion years were still around today, this planet would be jam-packed!

Plateosaurus (PLAT-ee-oh-SOR-uhss) was in a group of dinosaurs called **prosauropods** (pro-SAW-roh-pods), which disappeared in a background extinction in the Jurassic.

X OUT EXTINCTION

Extinction is a natural process that's a part of life, but there are also some extinctions that aren't so good for the Earth. People can cause an animal's extinction by hunting it or destroying the places it lives. Usually when this happens, there isn't a new species to take its place, so fewer and fewer animals are left. So people try to save animals that are going extinct because it's good for everyone, not just the animals that are disappearing.

Protoceratops

Extreme Extinctions

When lots of animals go extinct at the same time (like the dinos did), you get a *mass extinction*. Mass extinctions are very different from background extinctions, which you read about on page 10. Three things happen in a mass extinction:

◆ Many different types of animals disappear, or go extinct.

◆ The disappearances happen all over the world, not in just a few places.

◆ The disappearances take place in a short time period—a few thousand or million years. That might not seem short to you, but compared to the 3½ billion years since life appeared on Earth, a few million is just a blink of an eye!

HEY! WHERE'D HE GO?

You can use your **3-D glasses** to see two hidden pictures on this page. To see the first one, put on your glasses and close your left eye so you're only looking through the **blue lens.** Can you see the dino? To see the second picture, close your right eye and look only through the **red lens** of your glasses. What do you see now?

Gimme a K!

The extinction that wiped out the dinosaurs happened at the end of the Cretaceous Period and the beginning of a period called the **Tertiary** (TER-shee-air-ee), so scientists call it the **K-T extinction** for short. The K-T stands for **C**retaceous-**T**ertiary. (Scientists use K to stand for Cretaceous, since there's another time period that begins with C.) Even though the K-T extinction is famous for wiping out dinosaurs, they weren't the only things that disappeared. About half of all life on Earth went extinct!

Learning from Layers

Since people weren't around when the dinos said, "so long!," how do scientists know that they died in a mass extinction instead of a background extinction? Scientists get clues from studying fossils in prehistoric rocks. They find lots of dino fossils in almost all the Mesozoic rocks up to about 65 million years ago. But in rock layers formed right after the Cretaceous, dino fossils don't show up at all. If dinos did go through a background extinction, scientists would just find fewer and fewer fossils in rocks after the Cretaceous. So scientists know that something big happened that wiped out all the dinosaurs fast in a mass extinction.

THE BIG FIVE

The K-T extinction is the most famous mass extinction. But it's not the only one that has ever happened. Since the beginning of time, scientists have discovered five big mass extinctions, and some of them were bigger than the one at the end of the Cretaceous. Scientists have lots of ideas about what may have caused each of the extinctions, but they don't really know for sure. Turn to page 12 to learn more about these extreme extinctions.

WIPE OUT!

Percentage of plants and animals wiped out

| 10% | 20% | 30% | 40% | 50% |

Late Ordovician: The extinction that occurred 444 million years ago in the **Late Ordovician** (OR-doh-VIH-shuhn) only hit animals in the ocean, since they hadn't gotten to living on land yet. More than half of all species died. They were mostly small creatures, like **trilobites** (TRY-loh-bites) and **graptolites** (GRAP-toh-lites).

Trilobite

Late Devonian: Many ocean species living in warm waters said, "see ya!" in this mass extinction during the **Late Devonian** (deh-VONE-ee-uhn), which killed off nearly three-quarters of all life 360 million years ago. Animals that were hardest hit included corals, jawless fishes, and small marine animals called **conodonts** (CON-oh-dahnts).

Jawless fish

Permian-Triassic: The largest known mass extinction happened 251 million years ago at the end of the **Permian** (PERM-ee-uhn), about 30 million years before dinos showed up. Scientists think that only five percent of plants and animals managed to escape that one! Animals that got wiped out included armored fish called **placoderms** (PLACK-oh-derms), spiny-finned fish called **acanthodians** (A-can-THO-dee-ans), and animals like *Dimetrodon* (die-MEET-troh-don).

Triassic-Jurassic: At the end of the **Triassic**, 200 million years ago, a mass extinction hit land animals. While it wasn't so great for animals like **archosaurs** (ARK-oh-SORS) and **therapsids** (thayr-RAP-sids) like *Lystrosaurus* (LIS-troh-SOR-uhss), this mass extinction helped put dinos at the top.

Archosaur

Cretaceous-Tertiary: This was the extinction that wiped out the dinosaurs, as well as half of all the other life on Earth. What happened? Turn to page 14 and let's find out!

Triceratops (try-SER-uh-TOPS)

Tyrannosaurus rex

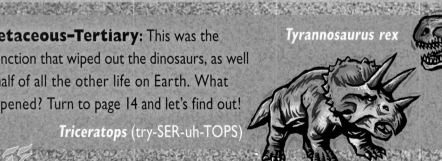

The K-T extinction wasn't the only mass extinction that's come around since life appeared on Earth 3½ billion years ago. Take a look at the chart below and check out the biggest mass extinctions of all time.

60%   70%   80%   90%   100%

Graptolite

Conodont

Placoderm

Acanthodian

Dimetrodon

Lystrosaurus

A VANISHING ACT

Ever since the first dino fossils were discovered, scientists have been trying to figure out what happened to these big reptiles. Scientists have lots of ideas on what caused this vanishing act. Check out these pages for the scoop.

A Spacey Idea

After years of wondering what on Earth could have wiped out the dinosaurs, some scientists began thinking about what in *space* could have done it. About 25 years ago, a group of scientists came up with a far-out idea. They said that a huge **meteor** (MEE-tee-OR) the size of New York City zoomed in from outer space and smacked right into Earth.

Big Blackout

While this meteor was BIG, it wasn't big enough to *squish* all the dinos on Earth. Instead, scientists think that when this space rock hit, it blew tons of dust and dirt into the air. This dust and dirt would've been so thick, it would've caused lots of changes in the weather and blocked out the sun, too. Without any sunlight, plants would've died. Without plants, all the plant-eating dinos wouldn't have had anything to eat, so they would've died, too. And without any plant-eaters to eat, meat-eating dinosaurs would've died as well.

Reading the Rocks

Scientists came up with the meteor idea after they looked at clues in the layer of rocks formed when the dinos went extinct, called the **K-T boundary** (BOWN-duh-ree). Check out the list below to see what they found:

◆ **Iridium** (ih-RID-ee-uhm) is a metal that's rarely found on the surface of Earth, but appears a lot in meteors. Since iridium would have fallen off the meteor as it hit Earth, scientists think the iridium layer in the K-T boundary proves that a big meteor did knock out the dinos.

Dino Dictionary

A *meteor* is a space rock that enters the air around the Earth. Most meteors burn up before hitting the ground, but the ones that crash into Earth are called *meteorites*. When a meteor hits the ground, it makes a large hole called a *crater*.

A giant space rock near Earth.

◆ **Quartz** (KWORTS) is a kind of rock that's found all over the world. When quartz is squeezed really, really hard, criss-crossed lines form in the rock. Scientists call this kind of rock *shocked quartz*. Scientists think shocked quartz formed in the K-T boundary when the giant meteor crashed into Earth.

◆ Since the meteor would have been super-hot when it hit, it would have melted certain kinds of rock to form tiny **glassy pebbles** found in the K-T boundary.

◆ With all the heat, the meteor would have also started big fires by burning up forests and other stuff. These huge fires would've made lots of black ash, or **soot** (SUT) that's found in the K-T boundary.

A BIG DISCOVERY

The crater at Chicxulub, Mexico.

Since the meteor crashed into the Earth at a super-high speed, it exploded as soon as it hit the ground. So instead of looking for pieces of the meteor, scientists started looking for a big hole, or **crater** (KRAY-tur), where it landed. In 1991, scientists found a big crater in Chicxulub (CHIK-soo-loob), Mexico, that was just the right size and made around the time when the dinos vanished. While some scientists think that this is the crater from the meteor that wiped out the dinos, others think it was made *before* the dinosaurs went extinct, so scientists still aren't sure if they've found the right one.

So it was the meteor, right?

A Hot Idea

Hold on! There's a whole other group of scientists who don't go along with the meteor idea at all. They think what killed the dinos wasn't something from space or even something that happened suddenly. Check out these pages for their really *hot* idea.

OOOH PRETTY!

An erupting volcano

Lots 'o' Lava

Scientists know for sure that at the end of the Cretaceous, there were lots of active **volcanoes** (vol-KAY-nohs). Some scientists think that over several million years, these volcanoes spewed enough lava, dust, soot, and poisonous gases to block out the sun and change the weather, just like a big meteor crash would. And just like you read on page 14, without sunlight, the plants, plant-eaters, and then meat-eaters would all die.

Dino Dictionary

A *volcano* is a mountain with an opening at the top that spews lava, rocks, soot, and poisonous gases. When this happens, it's called an *eruption* (ih-RUPT-shun).

More Rock Reading

So what clues have these scientists found in the K-T boundary for the volcano idea? Remember the iridium, shocked quartz, glassy pebbles, and soot layer on pages 14–15? The volcano-idea scientists don't think those things were from a meteor at all. They think all that stuff was caused by volcanoes. Let's look at those clues again:

◆ The metal **iridium** is rare on the Earth's surface, but there is iridium *inside* the Earth. Since volcanoes shoot out melted rock from deep within the Earth, that might explain how iridium got into the K-T boundary.

◆ Big explosions caused by volcanoes erupting could also have made the **shocked quartz** in the K-T boundary.

◆ When a volcano spews lava, some of it cools down and forms glass. So the **glassy pebbles** in the K-T boundary could also be from volcanic eruptions.

◆ Volcanoes also make lots of soot and ash. Millions of years of eruptions could have formed the **soot layer** found in Cretaceous rocks.

BLOWING ITS TOP

Deep inside the Earth, things really sizzle—it's so hot that rock melts! This melted rock is called **magma** (MAG-muh). Magma has gases that push it up toward the surface of the Earth. Sometimes the gases make

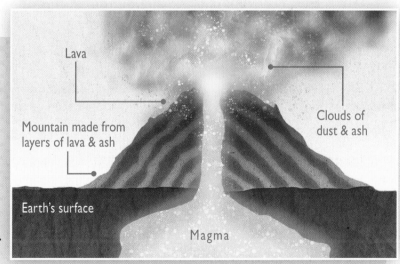

Lava

Clouds of dust & ash

Mountain made from layers of lava & ash

Earth's surface

Magma

magma explode or erupt out of openings at the surface where it becomes lava. As lava and ash spew out of the opening, they cool and form the cone or dome shape that many volcanoes have. Some volcanic eruptions are so violent that they blast ash, rocks, and poisonous gases up to 20 miles (32 km) into the air.

So it was a meteor OR volcanoes?

More Big Ideas

Wait, there's more! Even though the meteor and volcano ideas are the most popular, some scientists have come up with a few more big ideas on what made dinos go extinct. Check out these pages for more info.

Super Star

Dino Dictionary

A supernova is the explosion of a very large star.

One idea is that a star seven or eight times bigger than our Sun exploded in space. This **supernova** (SOO-pur-NOH-vuh) would have given off dangerous rays that hit Earth, killing dinosaurs and other kinds of life. While scientists think the supernova is a good idea, they haven't found any proof to back it up just yet.

Crazy Comets

Here's another spacey idea for dino extinction. Some scientists think that every 26 million years or so, a nearby star knocks into a cloud of comets that hang out at the very edge of our solar system. Scientists think that this same star knocked into the cloud at the end of the Cretaceous and sent lots of comets sailing toward Earth. And if you thought one meteor was bad, a bunch of comets are even worse!

A supernova blast wave

Warming Up

Scientists know that about five million years before dinos went extinct, some prehistoric seas started drying up as the Earth cooled and the continents

A comet sails past Earth.

moved. Since seas and oceans store heat from the air, they help keep the weather not too hot and not too cold. But as Cretaceous seas dried up, the weather began to get extreme. Scientists don't think that weather changes were the only cause of the K-T extinction, but along with a meteor or volcanoes, it could have helped wipe out the dinosaurs.

The Last Straw

Some scientists believe that dinos were already dying out before the mass extinction at the end of the Cretaceous. Giant fish-shaped marine reptiles called **ichthyosaurs** (ICK-thee-oh-SORS) and other reptiles had disappeared in background extinctions by the Late Cretaceous. So some scientists think that whatever happened—a meteor, volcanoes, or both—just helped finish off dinos since they were already dying out. But other scientists think that dinos were still going strong at the end of the Mesozoic.

GOOFY GUESSES

While there are lots of good ideas about why dinos went extinct, there are tons of silly ideas that people have come up with to explain this prehistoric vanishing act. Check out the goofy guesses on these pages.

THE GOOF: Dinos' brains were too small and dinos were too stupid to survive.

I DON'T GET IT.

THE TRUTH: While it's true that most dinos had small brains for their body size, these reptiles managed to survive for over 150 million years. That's way longer than humans, and we're the brainiest species around! If dinos were really so dumb, they would've died out millions of years earlier.

ACHOOO!

THE GOOF: Flowering plants appeared before dinos went extinct, so dinos must have died because they were allergic. Or, dinos ate the flowers and got bad stomachaches that killed them.

THE TRUTH: Flowering plants had been around for millions of years before dinos became extinct. So if flowers did kill dinos, they would've gone extinct a lot sooner.

I CAN'T GET UP!

THE GOOF: Dinos got so big that they couldn't move around without hurting themselves. Since they couldn't move, they couldn't find food, and they starved to death.

THE TRUTH: It's true that dinos got really big during the Mesozoic, but they'd been huge for millions of years before going extinct. Plus, scientists haven't found evidence of more injuries in dino bones from the end of the Cretaceous. And this goofy guess doesn't explain why small- and medium-sized dinos went extinct, too.

OH BOY!

THE GOOF: Aliens kidnapped the dinosaurs.

THE TRUTH: No one's been able to prove that aliens exist. And if aliens don't exist, there's no way that they could have been dino-nappers!

THE GOOF: Mammals ate all the dinosaurs' eggs.

THE TRUTH: Some mammals might have eaten dino eggs, but there's no way they could have eaten every single egg. And today's egg-eating mammals don't cause the extinction of egg-laying animals.

THE GOOF: Dinos drowned in their own poop.

THE TRUTH: Big animals can have pretty big droppings. But it just isn't possible to have that much poop build up!

THE GOOF: Super-hungry caterpillars ate all the plants, so there was no food left for plant-eating dinosaurs.

THE TRUTH: It wouldn't be possible for caterpillars, or any other animal, to eat all the plants. If caterpillars were such monster munchers, they would have caused the extinction of lots of leaf-eaters today.

THE GOOF: Temperature changes in the weather caused dino eggs to hatch as all girls or all boys. With only girls or only boys, dinos weren't able to have babies and died out.

THE TRUTH: It's true that crocodile and alligator eggs turn out to be boys or girls depending on how warm they're kept in the nest. But alligators and crocodiles lived alongside dinos and survived the extinction, so this reason doesn't explain why the dinos went extinct.

THE GOOF: As the continents broke apart and oceans disappeared, dinos crossed into new surroundings and lived with new kinds of dinos, too. Then the dinos caught each others' diseases and got so sick that they died.

THE TRUTH: Lots of dinosaurs were still on isolated continents at the end of the Cretaceous, so they hadn't met any new dinos with new diseases. Plus, this doesn't explain how all the ocean reptiles died out in the K-T extinction.

THE GOOF: Mammals ate all the dinosaurs' food.

THE TRUTH: Mammals and dinosaurs existed together throughout the Mesozoic. For the most part, they probably ate different foods. But even if they didn't, the dinosaurs would have gone extinct much earlier if mammals were eating all their food.

THE GOOF: Dino eggshells got too thin and kept breaking, so no new dinos were being born.

THE TRUTH: Some dinosaurs' eggshells were thin, but other Late Cretaceous animals, like birds and turtles, had thin eggshells, too. But some of these animals survived the K-T extinction, so it doesn't explain why the dinos didn't.

While scientists don't know for sure what caused the K-T extinction, they do know that it changed the world—and not just for dinos! On these pages we'll take a look and see who made it, and who went extinct.

Who Disappeared?

While the K-T extinction is famous for wiping out the dinosaurs, they weren't the only animals that disappeared. About half of all the species on Earth went poof! Check out the list below to see the animals that didn't make it:

◆ **Dinosaurs**. To see some of the dinos that were hanging around in the Late Cretaceous, turn to page 30.

◆ Flying reptiles called **pterosaurs** (TARE-oh-SORS).

◆ Big ocean reptiles like **plesiosaurs** (PLEE-zee-oh-sors), **mosasaurs** (MOE-suh-SORS), and very large sea turtles.

◆ Marine animals called **ammonites** (AM-uhn-nites), which were relatives of today's squids and octopuses.

◆ Big cone-shaped clams called **rudists** (ROO-dihsts) that made reefs like coral do today.

◆ Many kinds of **sharks** and **rays**.

◆ Many species of **marsupials** (mar-SOO-pee-uhls), animals that raise young in pouches on their bodies.

◆ **Birds** with teeth (today's birds are toothless).

◆ Many species of **plants**.

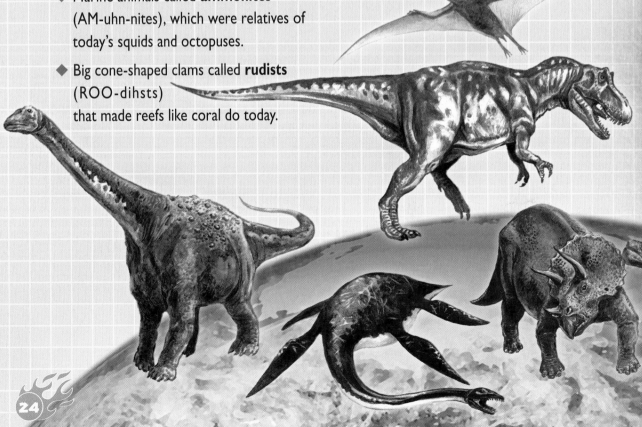

Move Over for Mammals

The extinction wasn't bad news for everyone. For **mammals** (MAM-uhls), it was the best thing that ever happened. During the Mesozoic Era, reptiles were the stars of the show, since they ruled on land, sea, and air. While dinos and other reptiles were enormous, Late Cretaceous mammals weren't much bigger than a house cat, and none lived in the ocean. But with dinos out of the way, mammals got the chance they needed to become the most successful group of animals alive today. Mammals had lots of company, too. See the list below for other animals that made it:

Dino Dictionary

Mammals are animals that are mostly covered in hair and give birth to live babies.

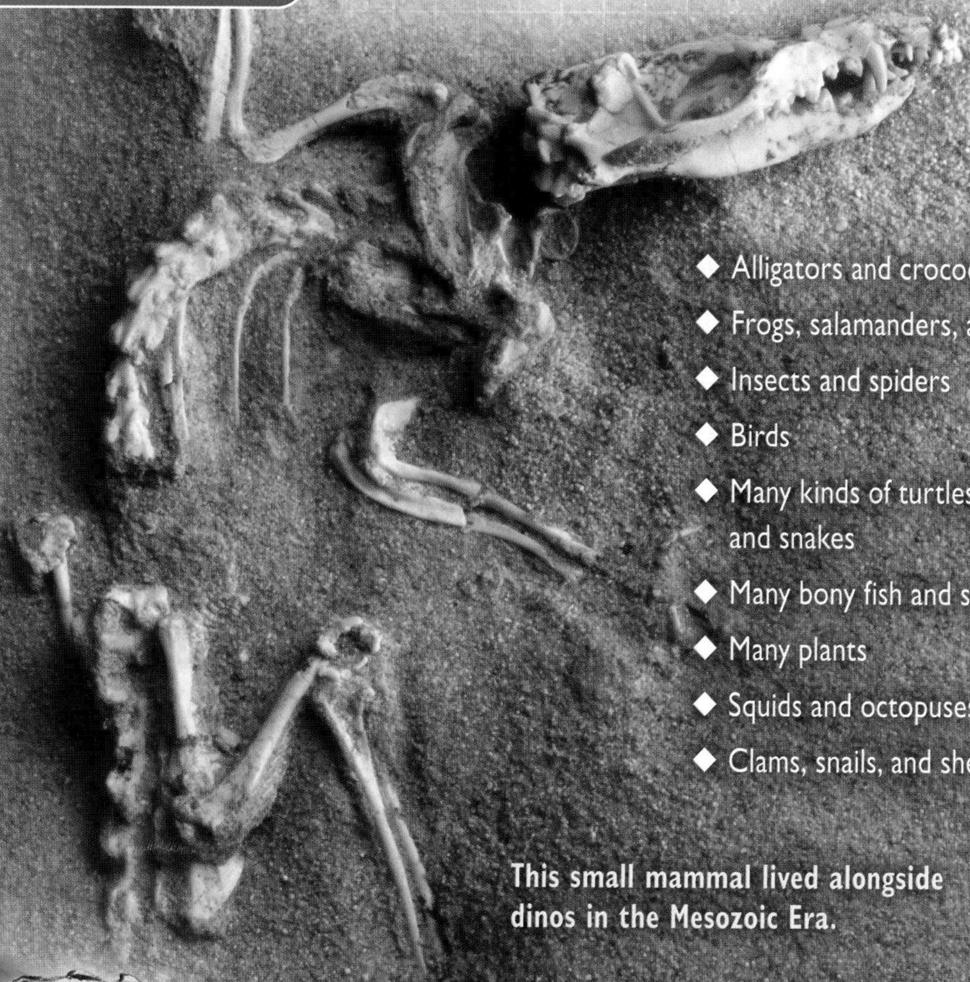

◆ Alligators and crocodiles

◆ Frogs, salamanders, and lizards

◆ Insects and spiders

◆ Birds

◆ Many kinds of turtles, lizards, and snakes

◆ Many bony fish and some sharks

◆ Many plants

◆ Squids and octopuses

◆ Clams, snails, and shellfish

This small mammal lived alongside dinos in the Mesozoic Era.

DINO DATA

Since mammals are the largest and most common animals today, many people call the time we live in "The Age of Mammals."

Survival Secrets

How did some animals manage to survive the extinction when so many others couldn't? Scientists don't really know, but they have some ideas.

Since many animals that survived lived underground in burrows, some scientists guess that this might have helped them. Others think that the animals that survived ate lots of different foods, while picky eaters died out. But some scientists don't agree with these ideas at all. It's another mystery waiting to be solved!

Living Dinosaurs

Are you sad that dinos aren't around anymore? Well, here's some great news. Some dinos are still alive and well. And you probably see them every day!

Wait a minute! I thought ALL dinos were extinct?!

Yup, dinos are still around. That's because modern-day birds are directly related to dinos. Here's the scoop: scientists believe that, over millions and millions of years, some small, meat-eating dinos adapted to help them survive their changing surroundings. They grew feathers, and their arms and hands became wing-shaped. This group of dinos eventually became birds that lived alongside dinos and survived the K-T extinction. While a flamingo might not be your idea of a dino, scientists put birds into the dino group. And since birds live on today, you can say that dinos live on today, too.

Can you see how this *Mononykus* (MON-oh-NYE-kuss) and this chicken are alike?

IF REPTILES RULED TODAY...

Gorgosaurus
(GOR-goh-SOR-uhss)

Have you ever wondered what life would be like if giant reptiles were still around? You might be surprised to see how different the world would be! Turn the page and see what might've happened if the K-T extinction had skipped town.

Ruling Reptiles

If there was no K-T extinction to wipe out dinos, that means that it would still be The Age of Reptiles. So along with dinos, you'd see big reptiles EVERYWHERE, including gigantic sea monsters and flying ones, too. Yikes!

Dino Dictionary

When an animal *evolves*, it changes slowly over time in order to survive.

Bring On the Dinos!

Did you know that there were lots more kinds of dinos at the end of the Cretaceous than when they first appeared on Earth? It's true! That's because for 150 million years in the Mesozoic Era, dinos kept **evolving** (ih-VOLV-ing) and new species appeared. So if dinos were alive today, there would be even more kinds since they would've had another 65 million years to evolve.

I Know That Dino!

Even though there would be more kinds of dinos, most of the dinos that you'd see would be pretty familiar-looking. That's because the most famous dinos (like *T. rex* and *Triceratops*) lived in the Late Cretaceous. While 65 million years is a long time, scientists don't think that dinos would have evolved to look a whole lot different than they did before the K-T extinction.

And you'd be a dino expert!

Missing Mammals

The Age of Reptiles wouldn't be good news for everybody. Mammals would seriously miss out, since the K-T extinction was their chance to become large and in charge. Scientists think that there probably wouldn't be many large mammals, like elephants. And the ones that managed to evolve would probably live in colder places, like the Arctic, since reptiles would be hogging all the warm spots. Since people are also mammals, scientists think humans would have missed their shot on Earth, too. Bummer!

No (Dino) Pets Allowed

Even if humans had managed to make it on Earth with dinos still hanging around, we probably wouldn't be able to make them into pets. Too bad…riding a dino to school might be a lot of fun! Instead, you might be able to visit a dino at the zoo or see them on safari. Cool!

PALEONTOLOGIST
GREG WILSON

Meet Greg Wilson, a mammal paleontologist at the Denver Museum of Nature & Science in Colorado. Dr. Wilson isn't an expert on dinos, but he is really interested in the K-T extinction. Why? Read on and find out!

Q If you study mammals, why are you interested in dino extinction?

A The K-T extinction was an important event in the history of life, not just for dinos. It was a chance for plants and animals that weren't as common, like mammals, to become more widespread. And the K-T extinction didn't just wipe out dinos—some mammals, like marsupials, were hard hit, too.

Q How do you use fossils to study the K-T extinction?

A Right now I'm looking in Hell Creek, Montana, for small mammal fossils, mostly teeth. We look at these fossils and try to figure out the changes that happened in mammals during different parts of the Late Cretaceous. By looking for changes in the number of different species, the numbers of animals within each species, and changes in body size, we can try to see if there were any warning signs that showed an extinction was coming, or if it happened suddenly.

Q Why do you think some mammals survived the K-T extinction, but not dinos?

A We don't know for sure, but we can look at the animals that survived to get an idea about what things might have helped. Back then, mammals mostly had small bodies, ate lots of different things so that if one kind of food disappeared, they wouldn't starve, and were warm-blooded (they didn't need the sun to keep warm). It's possible that these things helped them survive the K-T extinction, but there were also small dinos in the Late Cretaceous, and some people think that dinos were warm-blooded, too. So these things don't explain everything. And remember, birds are dinos, so dinos aren't completely extinct.

Q What's the funniest extinction idea you've ever heard?

A There's a joke that some flavors of JELL-O® have lots of iridium, so all the iridium in the K-T boundary was from a giant JELL-O® comet that killed the dinosaurs. It's not true, but pretty funny.

Dr. Wilson in the field.

THE LAST DINOSAURS

Right before the K-T extinction, lots of different kinds of dinos were still going strong in the Late Cretaceous. Read these pages for more info on the last dinosaurs!

One group of the last dinos was made up of big plant-eaters called **hadrosaurs** (HAD-roh-sors), like **Anatotitan** (ah-NAT-toe-TIE-tan), shown below. When *Anatotitan* was first discovered in 1882 in South Dakota, scientists noticed that this dino had a tough beak shaped like a duck's bill. So they started calling hadrosaurs "duck-billed" dinos, and the name stuck! Like all hadrosaurs, *Anatotitan* used its tough beak to snip off tough plants and branches and had hundreds of flat teeth inside its mouth to grind up these green goodies. Yum!

Another Late Cretaceous dino was **Pachycephalosaurus** (PACK-ee-SEFF-a-loh-SOR-uhss) which was named by the famous fossil hunter Barnum Brown in 1943. This dino had a dome-shaped head and a skull that was up to 10 inches (25 cm) thick. That's as thick as three phone books! Scientists think that *Pachycephalosaurus* used its hard head to push against the sides of other animals to defend itself or to find a mate.

Alamosaurus (AL-am-moh-SOR-uhss) was a giant plant-eater that was discovered in 1922. Longer than two school buses, scientists think that *Alamosaurus* was one of the biggest dinos back in the Late Cretaceous. *Alamosaurus* was part of a group of long-necked plant-eaters called

Tyrannosaurus rex

Triceratops

Ankylosaurus

titanosaurs (tie-TAN-oh-SORS) that appeared all over the world in the Cretaceous, especially in South America.

Horned dinos, like **Triceratops** (try-SER-uh-TOPS), were also some of the last dinosaurs alive during the Late Cretaceous. *Triceratops* was first found near Denver, Colorado, in 1889. Since then, over 50 *Triceratops* fossils have been found in the U.S., making scientists think that this dino was pretty common back in the Late Cretaceous. *Triceratops* and other horned dinos had big, bony plates on the backs of their heads called *frills* and parrot-like beaks to help them chew through tough branches. Scientists think that these dinos used their frills and horns to scare off hungry meat-eaters and find mates.

Another dino that lived all the way up to the K-T extinction was **Ankylosaurus** (ang-KYE-loh-SOR-uhss). This short and squat dino wasn't fast on its feet, but it was covered with bony plates growing out of its leathery skin for protection. It also had a big, bony club at the end of its tail that it could use to whack attackers! Since there were lots of huge and heavy meat-eaters looking for lunch in the Late Cretaceous, all that armor was probably a good idea!

The most famous dino of all time, **Tyrannosaurus rex** (tie-RAN-oh-SOR-uhss RECKS), also lived during the Late Cretaceous. *T. rex* walked on two legs and had big, sharp teeth to catch and chomp its meals with. It grew over 40 feet (12 m) long and weighed up to 7 tons. Scientists think that *T. rex*'s mouth could open super-wide—big enough to swallow an adult human!

Looks like a dino party!

Anatotitan

Alamosaurus

Pachycephalosaurus

GOING, GOING, GONE!

Well, the dinosaurs may be extinct, but the search for answers to this mystery lives on! We've looked at lots of clues scientists have found about the K-T extinction. And we've investigated some of the best (and worst!) ideas about why it happened. Keep on exploring and maybe you'll be able to solve this prehistoric puzzle someday!

Maiasaura (MY-uh-SOR-uh)